The Special Photo

Written by Jack Gabolinscy
Illustrated by Richard Hoit

Every day, I dived and took photos in the bay. At night, I checked them, printed the best and deleted the rest. I had some great photos in my album, but I was after something very special. I wanted a photo to enter in the Bay Photo Competition – a photo good enough to win the underwater camera that was first prize.

I had a photo of a giant brown sea turtle swimming in the bay. There was one of a pink and brown shell as big as a football lying on the bottom. I had one of an angry-looking eel halfway out of its hole. I had pictures of piper fish, poisonous jellyfish and a stingray gliding through the water like a giant grey and white butterfly.

3

My album had lots of good photos, but I needed something better. I needed one so different that nobody could beat it.

Every day, I searched the bay taking photos. At night, I printed the best and added them to my album. Sea snakes, dolphins, hermit crabs, schooling kingfish, parrot fish and pufferfish and many more. My collection grew, but I still didn't find the one I wanted.

On the last day of my holiday, I swam out to Big Rock. Face down, camera ready, I kicked through the water, searching the bottom. Once, twice, three times I went down, but there was nothing. I was ready to give up and go home. "One final lap," I decided. "If there's nothing, I'm out of here." I went down into the shadows.

And that's when I saw it . . .

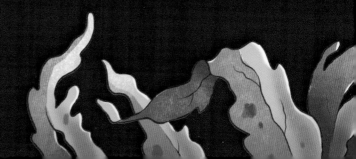

A large, dark shape was lurking in the gloom among the seaweed on the bottom. It was watching me. Its wide mouth opened and closed in a grin. I remembered the shark scare a week earlier. I yelled in fright. A burst of bubbles blew my snorkel out and, when I breathed back in, I swallowed a mouthful of water.

Back on the surface, I realised my mistake. It wasn't a shark. It was a big hole in the ocean floor. Long branches of seaweed growing out of it, swaying in the current, had made it look alive, and my imagination had turned it into a shark.

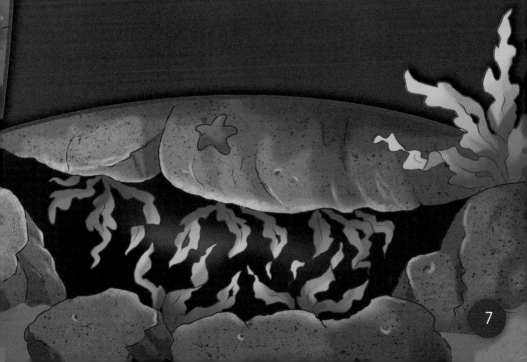

Even after I realised it wasn't a shark, the hole looked dark and spooky. I wondered how deep it was. Was it just a little pothole? Or was it a volcanic tunnel going all the way down to the centre of the Earth?

I dived down. My flippers and weight belt took me down quickly. The hole was as wide as my two arms could stretch, but I still couldn't see inside. It was all shadows and swirling weed.

I kicked again, down into the darkness, through the flapping seaweed. It slapped my face and wrapped itself around me.

I sWam On doWn into the darkness.

9

Suddenly, the seaweed let go of my legs. I was down in the hole. It wasn't dark and scary any longer. Instead, it was as bright and clear as daylight. Tiny, colourful fish swam about me. Starfish, sea slugs and crayfish clung to the rocky walls. Below me, the hole continued, dark as a train tunnel.

I was out of air. I couldn't hold my breath much longer. Flash! Flash! I took a couple of quick photos then kicked upwards, hard. I broke the surface, huffing and puffing through my snorkel like an old steam engine.

I dived into the hole many times, each time a little deeper than the one before. Looking down, it always seemed dark and scary. But when I got there and looked up, it was clear, bright and beautiful. I took lots of photos, but not the one I really wanted.

I made my last dive. Down I plunged, kicking hard through the leaves, down into the darkness. Down, down, down. I kicked harder and further than ever before. Then I stopped and looked around. That's when I got scared. There, looking back at me from the cave wall just above my head, was a big, black eye. It blinked like a lizard. It moved... **Half the wall moved.** And that's when I got really scared.

I was in the hole with a giant octopus.
And it was above me. I would have to swim past it
to get out. The eye watched me. The long arms, like
snakes, writhed around the wall of the cave as it came
out from its hiding place. The suckers on its tentacles
opened and closed as it came for me.

I screamed, kicked for the surface, and accidentally pushed the camera button, all at the same time. The light flashed. The octopus pulled back in fright. And, in that instant, I shot past it. Up through the hole. Up through the seaweed. Up to the surface.

I reached the top, gasping for air, heart beating, hands shaking. I turned to check below. My brain told me the octopus wouldn't follow me, but my imagination wasn't so sure.

15

I lay in the water breathing deeply, the sun warming my body and calming me down. Then I swam ashore to pack and go home, disappointed that I hadn't got my special photo, but glad to be alive. I could have been octopus lunch by now.

That night, as usual, I checked my photos. There was one of the spooky black hole in the ocean floor. There were a few from inside it. But there was one special one that I hadn't expected. It was a photo of the octopus, taken when I accidentally set the flash off in its face. Its eyes were wide open, its tentacles waving about in fright. The octopus was even bigger than I'd thought!

And it was a good photo. A special photo. A photo that might just win the competition!

The Special Photo is a Recount.

A recount tells . . .

- who the story is about (the characters)
- when the story happened
- where the story is set.

Who	When	Where
	on the last day of my holiday	

A recount tells what happens.

A recount has a **conclusion**.

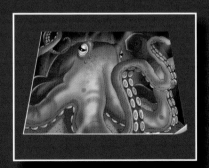

Guide Notes

Title: The Special Photo
Stage: Fluency

Text Form: Recount
Approach: Guided Reading
Processes: Thinking Critically, Exploring Language, Processing Information
Written and Visual Focus: Illustrative Text

- **Discuss with the students the importance of water safety and not swimming alone.**

THINKING CRITICALLY
(sample questions)
- What do you think this story could be about? Look at the title and discuss.
- Look at the cover. What do you think the swimmer has around his neck? Why do you think he has this?
- Look at pages 2 and 3. What kind of photo do you think would be good enough to win the competition?
- Look at pages 4 and 5. What do you think the boy might have seen?
- Look at pages 6 and 7. How do you think the boy feels about his mistake? Why do you think that?
- Look at pages 8 and 9. Do you think it was a good idea for the boy to swim into the hole? Why do you think that?
- Look at pages 10 and 11. What do you think the boy will do next?
- Look at pages 12 and 13. What do you think the boy has seen?
- Look at pages 14 and 15. Why do you think the octopus wouldn't follow the boy?

EXPLORING LANGUAGE

Terminology
Spread, author and illustrator credits, imprint information, ISBN number

Vocabulary
Clarify: album, eel, stingray, sea slugs, crayfish, tentacles, pothole, writhed, snorkel, jellyfish
Adjectives: *flapping* seaweed, *colourful* fish, *spooky* hole
Pronouns: I, it, me, my
Similes: gliding through the water *like a giant grey and white butterfly*, huffing and puffing through my snorkel *like an old steam engine*
Focus the students' attention on **homonyms**, **antonyms** and **synonyms** if appropriate.